I0152810

In and Out of Rough Water

In and Out of Rough Water

Poems by

Jayne Marek

Kelsay Books

© 2017 Jayne Marek. All rights reserved. This material may not be reproduced in any form, published, reprinted, recorded, performed, broadcast, rewritten or redistributed without the explicit permission of Jayne Marek. All such actions are strictly prohibited by law.

Cover photo: Jayne Marek

ISBN 13: 978-1-945752-29-2

Kelsay Books
Aldrich Press
www.kelsaybooks.com

To Joe, always, with love

Acknowledgments

Grateful acknowledgment is made to the residency program at Playa, where the poems for "Wheel of Orion" were developed. The author also thanks the editors of the following publications in which versions of these poems previously appeared:

The Bend: "After the Equinox," "Riverside Cathedral," "Snow Geese," "Windspace"
Backlit Barbell Anthology: "Yellow Rail"
Cincinnati Writers Project Anthology 2012: A Few Good Words: "Things I Want," "The Tree Surgeon Dreams of Bowling"
Community Breeze (Summer Lake, OR): "The Buckskin"
Company of Women: New and Selected Poems: "The Buckskin," "Burn Series," "Quality Control," "Range in the Stars"
Creative Colloquy: "Flavor of Roses"
Gravel: "Icicle"
Imposition of Form on the Natural World: "A Flash of Scarlet"
Lantern Journal: "Nothing Is Given" [excerpts]
Playa: On the Edge of the Great Basin: "High Desert Stars"
Prism: "The Farthest Point: Rock Island," "Time of Drift"
Tipton Poetry Journal: "Down," "To Ask Me"
Trailhead: Literature of the Backcountry: "Nothing Is Given" [excerpts]

Table of Contents

Part IV: Things I Want

About the Author

Part I: Time of Drift

Time of Drift

Long-drawn and tasty as Kentucky vowels
this sky has ridden with us for miles
of mild December morning

just a little old at the edges
where paper fields pull away from dry paste
darkened around the cut

pictures from old magazines loose now
cheap newsprint, gray and bone scraps blown
limp under the hands

of roadside burning bush, cold past color
except in subtleties of midwestern winter
a sun-touched spot

of earth raises a small balding scalp
leached grass carefully combed to the tips
—*goin' to meetin'*—

on a morning of oatmeal and milk-mixed clouds
—*bringin' our hymnbook with pictures in*
to keep him hush—

the old child who never grew old
but bent like rusty stubble in cornfields
bluntly cut

year after year the harvest passed
one late autumn the world locked up
drifted deep

into the white prairie of sky
the white roads of grain where he
wouldn't come to harm

all the seasonal pages of snow and sun
for forty years now darkened
by turning thumbs

Icicle

An icicle grows like a fang
From the roof eave of a person
Who does not like me.

He does not speak to me
But I see him standing
By the icicle, admiring it

For its efficient
Shape, as long as it needs to be
To get to one's heart.

Weak sun stretches the tip
To a point so narrow
One can see the future through it,

The horizon, hills that have fallen away
From each other, that
Broke the earth.

What a sound, I imagine,
The splitting and falling.
But this wrist of ice

Is thick and strong,
Grips the roof edge,
Makes my opponent smile

As he whispers
To the silent frozen water,
Praises its cruel gleam.

Range in the Stars

For a moment I drift into the photograph of distant mountains
at dawn, lavender peaks afloat above another ridge, dark purple,
the whole sky dusted with pink, the nearer landscape in maroon,
its tree and cactus shapes emerging. The January cold of Arizona
surprised me during my first visit, held me in a clinch. I learned
to love that cold as my mother loved this mountain range,
the Sierra Estrellas. She could sense how every day
the mountains breathed far away, rising from either side
toward a single crest above the dry Valley of the Sun.
Even hidden by smog, some days, the mountains were there,
her privilege, a place she would go to some day, she said.
In the photograph, the range gently draws a line
between lingering gloom and the rising light.

A Flash of Scarlet

A last young cardinal pips in the leafless
pear tree to say he's finally all red
after his dull rust-green adolescence,
but it's too late—no other cardinals stayed
to see in the winter. Puffs of snow rise
slantwise from under bare bushes, as if
called up from frozen ground by the bird's voice,
to be seen, seen! and fulfill a given life.

Winter will win, its whiteness pitiless,
and the red bird, vivid on naked twigs,
will draw the ragged harrier that floats
over a nearby field. The hawk's eye will fix
on this brightness, sweet as fiery berries
spilled across ice, singing its own red throat.

To Ask Me

I will listen to what he says
in the poem of water and winter,
the ice crust of his judgment.
Wet branches drag into the sweep
of drifts, skirting the oldest tree
in its heaviness of heart. What he meant
shifts all the land around me,
a cold blue wind.

But who can say that hate or love's
what swings the ice-bound branches
overhead? Can I trust him?—
that secret-heart, that man
of miles of blank fields pressing snow-fences
as if to flatten them—
the truth's what the black bird says

on its wire:
a path is itself and nowhere.
What our feet can grip,
we may not see. So move.

Lured into Glass

Secret messages in skyscraper windows flicker
Like passing wings as the days decline
Or open into sun. At a breathless
Height, metal edges hum,
Leafless and slim, offering
Illusory rest. Winds circulate
Pigeons, starlings, the junk birds
That city-dwellers hate, house
Sparrows pecking for meager food,
And their kin, buntings, warblers,
Flycatchers, siskins, towhees, swifts,
Finches and lovely robins.

But a cloud slides swiftly with long
Wings and startles a flock into a burst
Of feathers beating escape. Or
In the night, false stars dot the sills
And dust-clumps reflect street lamps,
Beckon like a sky, an open bowl
Of invisible stone. The sharp stop,
The slide, the fall, all the beautiful
Dead at the buildings' feet, come dawn.

Poem in Hyde Park

—for P.H.

Do you still live? says my surprise.
I remember the dark car drive with your voice
babbling your drink, the ocean you were in so deeply

over your head. Fingertips brushed
against the Craftsman woodwork of a living room
in Hyde Park, its lamps with only one bulb

lit. A rose color glowed,
there were strange people, elbows smelling of closets
that smelled of wool, a fallen gamy cap

in tweed. There must have been cheese underfoot.
Outdoors in the damp stood black
leafless trees streaming with self-righteousness,

crows shouting out parking directions
from the gables. Everyone was trodden
flat like November grass

at a corner of the yard.
One hand lifted and talking continued,
the air around me stifling with the body breath of booze.

The Farthest Point: Rock Island

Up on Rock Island, your feet
go on dead paths that follow
the broken molar crest of this island
like beadwork
along seams of supple leafskin.

You go west.
It feels natural to seek the blunt
end of things, the mess of boulders
under nettles and poison ivy,
place of black flies
that torment you through thin clothing.

It's hard going
through swarms of ancient spirits
no one remembered
to tell you about. You pass
empty brown bones of trees and enter
the guilty meadow.

A lighthouse of pale stone
deflects all the weather
riding in on wild west winds,
blunt as truth breaking passion.
No one lives here now.
Dozens of bites sting the beads of sweat
along your hairline,
your shirt is a cape of quills.
No place is clean,

so you stay on your feet.
It's a small island, after all.

Along the same path returning
the flies fall away in hundreds,
then dozens. You have forgotten
what you wanted to see.

In the distance,
white boats crowded with people.

Not Flight

Today your plane lifted off
The difficult runway of the quotidian
Into long clouds
Like underwings of red-capped cranes
Escaping to the north.

Envy punished my shoulders all day
Heavier than I remembered,
Twisting me under
That tightly built cairn
Of what is not.

I would be better off
Silent, at rest, as a petal
Spent on the grass.

Riverside Cathedral

It is too high for defense
and so it speaks
idealism: the other sense

What a Gothic tower,
opening above square streets
its deep-set collar

*

After years apart
we are jealous now
for each other's time

and walk together
the old ways
of your new city

gray as the granite
walls of college
days years ago

here in the open
streets the November wind
snatches our words

and wails of the world's
regrets around the steps
of the church

*

The baby your son cried
and cried, accepting
no comfort

his whole body
tinged with morning sky
pink and blue

his heart starving
from its own gift
to itself

blood to blood
channeled a new way
a moon-shaped eye

in the heart, and you said
God could have prevented this
and didn't

what then is love
that rocks and rocks the broken
to silence them

*

Entering the empty nave
we find the story windows
like daylit jewels

and scattered letters
of light rolled between the spindles
of candles

and stop for a time, quivering
with the beat of breath
over our hands

like syllables
we repeat to one another
in those moments

we forget, after long study,
that this is
a strange language

*

Now, we ascend,
we have agreed
to ride in the dark box

of the elevator
that plunges upwards
toward the belfry landing,

a mass of stone and cables,
all the earth
opened beneath

here are saints
etched in the tense
hollow wall of each bell

their hands lifted,
not stretched out to help,
a self-held piety

upheld by columns of air,
it seems the weight
of these mouths tolling

could pull
the whole thing
down

*

Vast space below our feet
the enormous bells silent
the supports groan

half a name spoken,
you grip the rail
can go no farther

on the catwalk woven of holes
through which the wind tears
with its mouth open

mocking those
who hesitate
one step at a time

*

Now alone amid
the colonnades
of variant light

I stare into the faces
etched in steel
as with titanic pins

the saints' feet fainter
like shadows
along edges of stone

upheld by faith,
heart reaching over the bricks
and iron grips

the unsmiling figures
watch with eyes fixed
by their knowledge

as if human still
awaiting the hour
they will lean into the wind

*

You refused this sight
even though fear
was shared between us

I cannot say
why I came to
this space

the catwalks hollow
the bells, the supports
anchored

so that the heavy swinging
when it comes
is accepted

even the air-sway
of this great tower
accounted for

the shadow moving
slightly across the roofs
a hundred feet below

regular as rhythm
inside a body
and required

*

For me to tell you
this presumes
too much

for what do I know
about the real
standing inside

the shadow of the real,
crossing the sidewalks
full of people

all moving
but the pattern fixed
it seems

each person a syllable
the rows of them
scattered

from here, what the eye
discerns
flows and separates

the inflections clear
to eyes that have learned
to read the figures hung

in blank light
inscribed in bright shards
and raised into view

*

I waited for you
you say, the words
echoing from the landing

where the windows pore
over the fearsome vacancy
of the world

far below, not so open
as the caged belfry walks
from which I descend

to find you, to find
the body of the voice
the bravery

that shames me,
acceptance of fear
that goes in grace

*

We descend, sharing
the silent fall of the elevator
through the tower's core

and emerge
onto regular streets
yet the seams

of the sidewalks, and the gray
crevices between stones
of the cathedral

are like scars
drawing a whole closer together
a kind of healing

after violation, a mark
that runs from breast to belly
in gray flesh

*

You have shown me
the clean stigma
of the skeptic

understanding
the whole that upholds
the hollow

and the closure
of one time
in the opening

of another,
the sacrifice of faith
in the waiting

I would not have known
but in your words
scattered by wind

you have told all
of your son
and the life he bore you

Heaven Opens Its Door

—in memory of Pete Seeger (1919-2014)

After a long concert, the musicians
Stood aside, talked quietly. One
Stroked mandolin strings, a loving touch.
The voice of the instrument hummed
Its familiar tone deep into each mind,

And the woman fiddler picked it up,
Plucked as on a banjo for a riff
That everyone knew. Her eyes closed,
Her hair, almost colorless in the late-room
Lamplight, sifted over her tilted head.

A human voice followed the tune,
Held it, as if pedaling a piano,
Long enough for the bassist to brush
The string that resonated too
As the guitarist slowly slung his box

Around to his belly, leaning, hands
Finding their weary accustomed places
With a joy past exhaustion. It was
Too late now. All the rest thrummed
With instrument or voice or slid the spoons

Together with soft rhythmic clicks
Through and through the folk band's favorite song,
For each other, late past late, harmonies
They felt in bones and breath and ear,
Until heaven opened its door.

Quality Control

Once in a factory
with machines in one room and
metal pieces and box forms in the next

where I sat with the
other women checking
hundreds of toothed white wheels an inch

across, listening
to the Lebanese woman calling us all
crazy—*shedonna*—the feminine ending—a noise

from the packing
area tables, like the box
stapler thump only gentler,

was the head and then
a scuffling sound, the feet of an older
woman down against

the two-by-four table legs
that hemmed her in
in the blue afternoon time under

long hanging lights too
poor to show either what you're working
on, or true shadow—

believe me, if you know
someone cheap, you know the light there—
she struggled for

twenty seconds in what
had to be filth, and then the men
from the punches pushed

up the machines' levers one
after another and hurried
over to cradle

her head and bumper
her arms during the rest
of the fit, but

the manager
        who always watched us women
no matter the work, wouldn't
let us get up. As if

his saying, "It's taken care of"
made that true, as if any words can
take or make

more than the eye with its
parallax
of encroachment

and calculation. You don't
know who will at last
see you in the slant

darkness of your own making.
Shedente, the Lebanese woman
whispered, flicked her wrist.

Part II: Nothing Is Given

Nothing Is Given: A Poetics of Place and Loss

Prologue: Tahoma

Fledged and shed in a rhythm of wind descends
the snow, groomed out like feathers from the ends
of an osprey's ruff, white around its neck
as rugged skirts of glaciers lined with rocks,

dress suited for the climate. For the climber,
the one who struggles, for the skier
or snowshoer, for anyone whose means
brings to this pass the faulty human frame,

the ordinary is the greatest burden
as scarf and hair and breath mingle and freeze,
weighting every step with all this world,

and, worst, the sufferer can well imagine,
as lungs labor to breathe amid needle ice,
there's but one step to go before the void.

The Cold Seasons

> *Limitless and potential, a kind of space*
> *Where one dissolves to become a part of something*
> *Entire….*
> *—Robert Pinsky*

A hike above treeline is baffled
by rocks left each season
in new patterns. The young

woman unafraid of the rigors of climb-
ing admires the shining
snags of ice-canopied

weeds that encase meadows in glass tubes, as
white and false brightness
rimes streambeds and seals up

the sky. Cold staggers down scree beds, heavy-
stepping in the early
autumn of altitude.

Creation moves backwards through a pass,
a denial of the promise
summer posed not long

before, when flaunted the elegant
flexible sweet-scented
cypress and white pine needles and, spread and lazy,

a hoary-furred marmot
that whistled to birds and did not get up
when she approached. But now

the beautiful, its fine bones scattered
on the gravel slopes of the mountain, shows
to be the broken

front faces of glaciers
that leak at the edges
and spit black rocks. The poetry

of descent and experi-
ment fissures words that tumble
downhill (so hard this mountain-

climbing) in haste in dwindling
color as shadows flex across ridges.
Now comes the question

of what has been done and
what is to be done, here
where one does not belong.

*

Winter so early at this elevation.
Ice drags each upright shape,
a calamity of ice.

Not to know whether there will ever be release,
whether
the chatter of iron-scented water will ever

be freed again, so late,
at the distant end of June.
The terrible surface winds

scrabble and squall, snow blooms
on the beaten branches, ten feet
above the spring-frog in its

stupor of mud—a creature
used to long darkness, its dream song
humming patience,

a trust without knowledge, without promise,
a trans-
mutation of minerals it can breathe.

*

White sky is water withheld until it decides.
The rumor of it
        drifts the year long.
Do not trust the distant visible ridge.

Somehow this earth stays closed, not persuaded
to air despite the water's probing,
its delicate, daily work.

In Spite Of

> *We hit her with little blows*
> *like an egg for peeling.*
> *—Yehuda Amichai*

A finger dragged on a desktop, pointing
to what ends a sentence:
an empty cartoon balloon, a simian grimace.

The box of words
fallen asunder
becomes axe handles.

*

A person abandoned by hope
feels the river inside
precipitate its thousands of years of silt

all at once, pressed into broad
rock with lavender stripes.
As if water still passed over it.

*

It's one's responsibility to criticize.
Push, push at words, force them to turn
or fall open under hothouse eyes.

Fit them to the polity, fit them
to yourself secondly. Don't
forget, you are here to please.

*

On a hill's crest, metal and brick buildings
built with the illusion of understanding
human life with a whole heart

rest on a gravel slope.
Underneath, slight shifts and adjustments
as every day pebbles press

and jimmy together and sand trickles
in spaces between and slips
deeper along paths of groundwater,

pipes, sewer lines, conduits
in black sheaths where voices
and water and sparks gossip underground,

by fractions undermining what's above, a pebble at
a time. One word, an emphasis, an epithet
louder than another knocks

loose a chip of mica
from rock that presses fiber-optic
cables bound in place in the deeply mixed foundation

of the lawn on which a man walks
in an illusion of consistency,
thinking he knows that on which he sets his feet.

*

The man's glance skips across the littered desk under an eave
(the renovated office-house is not kept up well) (windowsill
two tones of worn) past smudges on window panels, outside
tangle of branches, his words clog and then flow around leaves
crushed wet at the side of the street

(it will be possible years later to recall how black twig ends
of the maple gleam, each with a water drop at the end of its grip,
and to know exactly the chill that seeps under bark, freezes
and splits (not the intuitions but) the failing words, twisted,
wet brown, that lift at the edges but, too heavy,
cannot rise in an autumn gust) so many they smother the grass

*

The fugue of work over and over in your mind as if you know
nothing else, as if that will save you when the time comes that
someone doesn't like a word you said or the fact that you have
thoughts other than the fugue of work

over and over in your mind if the time comes someone doesn't like
you, and the hand closes into a fist so will not have thoughts other
than that you are nothing a fact of work not a person with a mind
that works as if that

were nothing, as if someone thinks time has come to nothing,
the fugue of work a fist closing over and over as if you have done
nothing that will save you when someone doesn't like facts or your
thoughts and closes then it is over

in your mind someone is a word you don't like, and time comes
like thoughts over and over closing around what one could have
said as if you know nothing else
as if that would have saved you the fugue the work
as if it were all nothing

*

After the ruin,
the giving up.
Still, things must be done.

Rain all morning traps a few dry spaces.
To be anywhere is difficult.

When days press tightly,
even air resists—
there's need to breathe—

the next and the next breath all suffer.
A dracaena bends toward a north window.

The side that is protected
distorts growth. Beware
what you think you want.

*

A word with you who think
the world's bare of love.
      Rain
does not stop one foot off the ground.

But fear,
      that gate gapes in full swing.
Its hinges whine
so loudly it turns every head.

*

Always hope—
      that high ceiling
may crack at its joints.

Wipe the insides of windows clean.
Can two drops meet if they both slip down—
      no, they are lost.

*

What does the water want us to do?
  —Yehuda Amichai

Count every salal-berry and leaf drawn by rain,
every thorn of rampant blackberries that
        force their footholds,

count the pointing fronds of ferns taller than oneself.
Count, heap the measure of twilight until
        a great horned owl admits its intent,

then hurry over the matted leaves   it is too late.

*

Set out   travel a gray road   the Dall's porpoises
        with white and black shoulders leap past the ferry

and bow under   the wren's song of pine-scents
as if you understand

In ringed black eye of a loon see the spirit
        and in a harbor seal swimming its head lifted

in water danced by grebes and storm winds
        along an archipelago of round stones

First there is the mountain then
there is no mountain
        what you once had is gone   this is a dying

*

Tenacity
broken logs cast all along the coast
        a few trees angled standing

*

The morning after storm
sky and surf
     resistant
     yet together

if that's not love   what will be

*

I always wanted to rest under
the long skirts of deodars

*

Words sift one's mind—
"I have drawn a circle round it"—

     a tear blot

     having fallen on a page
     of a book suddenly opened to new knowledge—
to give it some defenses.

For Getting Back

   and where are we, finally? Don't
   say that—we are nowhere
   finally...

   What I saw was rough, and still
   pains me. Perhaps it should pain me more.
   —Geoffrey Hill

Still waiting for word of welcome?
No one has welcome. The right place satisfies,
like long labor of a mind grown
older, and wild, as the tangles
of stunted pine limbs at treeline.

Can one live beyond here? Say no,
as if that will prevent a new
young pine from sprouting in such ground,
never knowing friendlier land
or ease of full growth. Say you know

that injustice can be seen more
than anyone likes. Say you
saw seedlings in mountain summer—
in bog or broken shale—reach for
day that was not yet turned to storm,

see whether that works. Certainly
there's always hope. You learn
how each thing wears itself away
against another, so stubborn
that endurance seems just nature.

*

To go up the book.
Roped, helmeted, rock-
booted, you will climb

the corner in the mountain
wall where the two faces form
a right angle, one

51

in shadow, one in sun
this morning, with each crack
in the jagged striae dark

where light folds
over stone—the good
finger- or toe-holds

you can see as you plan
the route—or, where light falls
into creases, invisible,

treacherous, too slim
perhaps to give a sure grip.
You start up.

*

To go back to where you fell
        from the page, to
re-read the hardest words, beyond understanding,
with understanding

is a gift of patience
        and of age.
These are the hardest words, beyond understanding.
So little matches up so.

*

The mountain is sustained,
its deadliness its nature,
its delicacy also its nature.

To know it well—for
its cruelty—is to have stiff red
feet nearly frozen from walking miles of mud

paths in the wrong time of year,
to take off one's boots in shouting cold
and massage numb toes with raw fingers.

Gray scarves blow ragged
in the couloirs.
To know what it means one must do this. Or

be too close to sun in bald
summer, no hope for any water
in baked land above the twisted

rim of treeline, where one watches thick cloud
banks from the coast cross the leading
ridges and hit the shimmer

of rising heat that
sucks them to vanishing wisps—any path here
is a path of excess. The idealist brings her human
body this way, nearly kills it.

*

> *For history's a twisted root*
> *with art its small, translucent fruit*
> *and never the other way round.*
> *—Paul Muldoon*

The mountain makes its own weather.
Not often seen, it becomes

53

fog that thickens in a certain
spot, even when the rest of the
sky's clear. In many days' gray rain

counted thrice over, the real seems
hidden in the proof that it's present—
a massive summit rounded from
past eruptions that gouged the swaths
now scarred with rough gray ice, glaciers

sunk by bad weather, rotting trunks.
If clouds part, one hour in winter,
the rare, sharp sight of the cap trimmed
white and blue seems illusion—there
always the impossible climbs.

*

> *what you'd / done to stay alive…*
> —James McMichael

> *You are not ready? You áre ready. Pass….*
> —John Berryman

To rappel; to be as if alone.
Still as a heelstone poised atop a ledge
scuffed by wind, stand, with a blue rope drawing
away from the body toward a safe covert
where the belay man can brace his legs
amid this clifftop's broken teeth. He in his white
helmet is ready, wheedling the sun

with an old pop song. Face him, step back,
one boot, other boot, steady that blue line, voice of the guide
walking this body back foot by foot, until gravel gives

under one boot and the other swings wide
before its toe finds surface. Bend knee, place the dangling
boot flat on the rock wall, the impossible rise,
awkward now the other foot dangles—
a foolish crane angled to the horizontal—

heavy head and shoulders sway
in open space to sink through as if forever.

One arm behind the back,
body so solid it drags
like a ship going down finally, its bellow stacks cracking,
the hand in front rolled like a ground squirrel, shadow-
striped, blue rope blistering, the two faraway brown boots
mapping uneven shale breaks,
something holds

in the tension of the cradle arm
as the wall crawls up toward the sky, scree scattering
messages into hollow echoes of helmet-held
breathing, blood beating, on on on, something's
holding, this body is holding, as if
a controlled fall won't last for years, as if
this quarter-turn of the map shows the world as it is.

Epilogue

Tempting to see the essence just as this:
one finds oneself through folly, and the world is
cruel, its forms, its seasons, unfriendly
and—wrapped deep, in the core—necessary,

and destiny means making the false
steps, the hard climb leading only to
the hard way down—that is to say, all ways.
Nothing is given: all that is true.

The mind is an exculpatory storm,
wind scouring all the shivering places
just as the poets promised, and one comes

to become the paths that lose and create
themselves again, in mind. As twilight closes,
a dark complex joins in shimmering routes.

Part III: Wheel of Orion—High Desert Poems

The Navigator

—for W. S. Merwin

Reading poetry in tercets and caesura forms
brings to mind your impatience
as you wrote in a book I owned
fixing a publisher's error
and my memory

of your hand bony as your face
writing a word more vivid than the print
on the mild page
unaware of its offense

years later when I open the book again
the bird in the palms is bathing
while outdoors a harrier winnows pale weeds
its flight like the shape of hills
in the distance

where hummocks mark the site of the oldest human habitation
that we know of in this place
in our paltry understanding
in these days of haste

one must find one's way
erratically
aware of whoever is watching
but needing to hunt
to eat and leave fragments in the grass

High Desert Stars

Winter night in the basin reaches for miles
toward ridges
that hide their ancient names

how few watchers will pay with cold
bones that feel like standing up in death
for an hour in the blackness

to see the stars
offered one coin at a time
as if hoarded for millions of years

while earth remolded itself time and again
never holding still

some stars are so dim
one doubts one's eyes
as one should

and the colors
blue and sepia gold silver and green
the pebbles in this river of space

into which one may wish to fall
sink ever more deeply seeing more and more
that takes the breath away

no one can reach this rainbow's end
it is futile
what is everlasting

is deep space that chills the foolish body
makes me glad
someday I will die

if only it could be like this
I hope death was so
for those I love now gone

The Buckskin

Along the high desert road
I came solitary
my breath a harsh signal
of the altitude as I ran
slowly
creating the only sounds not made by wind
and dry grass

passing a paddock I noticed
the horse as it noticed me
its black tail and ears raised
it snorted
and stamped
surprised by the unfamiliar human running

it understood
motion if not reason
feet drumming
we went the same direction
for a time sharing the wind

it outpaced me
turned and came around again to run
at my shoulder
as if to guide me toward
a road ahead
a road not yet perceived

at the fence it stopped letting me go
I wanted its thoughts
to follow me for a mile
around the base of the bluff

and more distant
places where I will be
remembering
looking forward together

No One to Answer

Will someone knock on this wooden door
more loudly than the hammer of wind from a ridge
to the west the land of evening of fading life

will a high hawk's cry and owl's hoot render
my name amid sticks and pine needles
as February folds its hands

why are there still fruits on the ground for evening
grosbeaks to pick over like yellowgreen beads scattered
after a fortune has been told

what flying so near my window suddenly banks
over the leafless tree with its dark buds
naked against the sky

Drinking Stone

Hollows come from many causes
      water dripping over thousands of years
onto one spot
      that cannot defend itself

a person could have bored into this stone
      using it as a prop
for a tool of another purpose
      the hollow resulted all the same

if neither from intent nor happenstance
      then we may say
the stone itself wished to harbor
      this deep open core

being uncovered
      its earth jacket crumbling
and washing off
      and surely this rock has fallen

or slid and struck rock elbows
      exposed to the elements
kicked by a passing deer
      along a trail that animals have always known

and that people followed to find animals
      in all weathers stumbling
on steep uncertain footing
      this little stone

did its part
      with its undulant topography

and now I think the hollow
        at its center may be

from a broken bone
        or orb of a bird's skull
a fossil within fossils
        there are patterns as of tiny shells

pocks where ancient mud accepted rain
        then hardened
leaves and seeds perhaps
        stalks of stiff grasses

that never bent over
        not even in death
the hollow in the rock's middle
        shaped the surface under it

that fits in my palm
        covers the lifeline's long creases
life be long
        stone be stone

yes I will drink from it
        it holds only a few drops
for me
        but can fill again ten thousand times

What We Love Must Be Left

Here there is so much weather
    clouds climb over ridges and tumble toward the basin
        the knobby meadows

ages in the making
    are shaped by rain and snow and especially the wind
        that caresses with urgent hands

it calls from so far off
    it can do nothing else

we learn these things while alone
    each knowing and trusting
        in love that looks in and out

to discern
    what is underneath the petals of our love

what grips the earth just below the surface
    what reaches out, believing
        there will be water, there will be sun enough

soil will not crack and ride off on the wind
    leaving the roots to dry death

that happens to some

the land here has learned to endure
    its hundreds of square miles cupped by rocks
        and open to the stars

Passed By

The clouds do not stay close to me—
by the time I look out the window
they are hurrying off,
having already gathered over my cabin.
I was not ready,
the wind complains.

So much rides away overhead
while I pull back the curtains
and fumble with the door latch,
exhalations from the high ridge are flowing east,
they shove my shoulders when I step outside,

tree limbs and tall grasses bow at this passing.
They feel what is given by the wind, the sky—
and where was I?
In my mind—
Wait for me next time, I say, and as my words
whip away the pines jostle and whisper—

Without You Is the Beginning of Winter

i.

From beginning to end the story appears on these pages
that touch each other's faces but cannot tell their tale
until the pages separate

someone is reading deep into the night
as snow accumulates outside against north walls
and curtains the other sides of windows

lamplight draws around the book
in the lap on the chair
that floats on waves that flow across the earth

the corners of the cabin gather whispers
snowdrifts arches of pages rising and turning
for hours or is it days or weeks

ii.

the earth goes dormant underfoot
gives no gauge for how long the time will be
grasses bed together unaware

rolled by snow they retain their shape after snowmelt
more storms will come to tread the contours of hills
deepen the fissures

the darkness under clouds mirrors the hills touches them
but pushes itself onward
night pacing into its emptiness

and each dawn pulls out long scarves in colors
of fire that overwhelms and consumes the sky
or of gray ashes that sift and vanish

winds speed down the western ridge
sounds of shale granite volcanic rocks collapsing
grinding themselves smaller

against the clamor of winter its unpersuadable agitation
this earth lies torpid huddled
for a long time cannot stir

iii.

the story is about how
I have left you
for the high desert

during this season of the wind
for so much need, so much power
I wish for the thing that could take me flying

across the eastern rim up to the stars that must be there

Windspace

I wear small earrings with chips of turquoise
      mounted along a twist of silver
in a style I have forgotten the name of
      made in the Southwest where my mother

lived much of the end of her life
      and my father too until he died
the crescent shape of the earrings is
      like swift air that carries away leaves

the pieces of turquoise are slivers of sky
      this stone made of sky
or the chips could represent people
      ancient marks on the walls of caves

showing the passing days years other things
      one wishes to remember
try to hold amid time's winds
      or rushing waters over bright

gravel that trickles in the currents
      follows the churning
riverbed for its miles
      the pebbles roll inches at a time

not knowing where they are going so slowly
      changing shape to get there
becoming smoother so that at the end
      one may think the journey was easy

it is not
      every collision every tumble under the surface
hard
      under the desert's eye so harsh

it brings tears
      my mother gave things to people to show
she was thinking about them
      once in a museum shop

we browsed separately companionably
      although she could hardly walk
she loved looking at jewelry of coral
      obsidian turquoise mother of pearl copper

and silver shadow box
      you can't be sure about the symbolism
said the shop woman
      shapes can mean different things

my mother chose for me these earrings
      while I wasn't looking
in those last days
      before the sound of winds rose in her mind

tearing words to shreds between rocks
      pushing her further downstream
where I could not reach her
      to say thank you I understand

Snow Geese

Urgent their necks and wings outstretched their wingtips
flicker black
      and their pale bodies
feint against buffeting wind
         they move so quickly
            into feathers of snow
one cannot count them whirring toward the horizon
                  as they turn and become one color
with the late day
      and now invisible
               sound of a beating heart

Yellow Rail

In late afternoon with shadows just beginning
to flow down ridges from the high cold west
slowly along the road I ran to a curve
at the end of the guardrail where I saw
water sipped the huddled feet of grass

and on the other side was a ditch of green
still water with edges of ice and old weeds
bent over in large hanks that could cover
a frog or bird who loved its secrecy
I heard a hinged voice

creak three times as if unaware of my human
presence quietly tracking the only road past
its hideaway both of us deep in the joy of
late February warmth and generous blue sky
and I stopped was that sound real yes

too early for frogs I thought when again
it creaked and then it seemed to sense I listened
we waited in an eternity of peace
I studied the shapes of shadows under bent staves
of bushes I followed the ditch with my eye

but the spell was not offered again
I seated myself on a guardrail pole to rest
and let the quiet minutes upon minutes gather
behind me unseen I could hear the rustle
of a mouse finding its way

I measured my breath as if I were the sky
tracing the crevices of the hillpoint
watched a cloud unravel to a wisp
two magpies came to quarrel in pine tops above
the road their wings a tumble of black and white

their cries like wires twisting they flew
when the birds had gone silence settled again
time turned slow pages in my thoughts
that before my birth I was alive
here in the ground in the remote passes

here in the brook's bubbles and in the east
the thin white lake toward which the water flows
here among volcanic rocks thrown
from earth into sky here is where they have fallen
cast under a late winter sun

this year brought me I found this place
on foot no one told me where to go
to hear what could be a rare bird hidden
amid the miles of rugged land I loved
the spell that had been offered only once

it became late the afternoon shadows turned gray
when I came to myself in the chill I rose to leave
no longer looking no longer listening
for more than the original blessing
the sun invisible behind the ridge's crest

Dead Zone (Burn Series I)

What if I were to climb the slopes of the mountains today
to find the place where light folds under the clouds
that skim the outcroppings this morning of half sun
and keep going letting the dimness surround me
lead me through damp weeds from rock to rock shadows
one at a time they become visible only when I move forward
and finally emerge higher into the daylight
where snow outlines stumps along ridges I have not yet climbed
I would be a transparent wing above the cloud line
among the dead trees marked by fire
touching their shells wondering why some burned black
and others white why some fell in crossed patterns
as if trying to escape to left or right
they all died but it was years ago and the quiet
fog has passed over them hundreds of times
concealing them an act of grace
I would move among the trees recognizing them
one by one alone and mute

Sunset Clouds (Burn Series II)

Huddled together the slide area hills give up their glow
and settle into tender slumber like chickens gathered on their shelf
quieting with a few murmurs as when wind traces a contour

through the pass between ridge and mountain
a wing of gold light unfolds along the flank of a hill near the top
amid the scarred trunks in the burned area that have not fallen
most bare and limbless

the dead trees remain at attention watching
signals of the sunset hidden behind western ridges tipped in pink
and violet   nothing else this evening except for

a cloud of green and yellow grosbeaks
dropping through black branches

Up There Day and Night (Burn Series III)

The dead stumps warn each other with their remaining limbs
     they signal for water
ready to carry it
     as if they were the multiplying brooms
in "The Sorcerer's Apprentice"
     lines of them rallying on the steep
slopes of charred pumice
     but no music begins
the ones that still have twigs
     reach in seventy directions
with witch fingers
     and like very old people sunken
into their own bones
     they do not mean to frighten
but the headless stumps
     did not survive
they trace on the sky night and day
     we did not survive

Your Birthday

Today is full of time, turning:
clouds of hard snow put one hand on the ground,
cartwheeling
between hawks sawing the wind
and perpetual grass bowing the way the weather goes—

toward you, far off
past the arid basin
that holds its breath and tries not to think
during the long privations of equinox season,
keeping a still mind.

I know water springs from the western hills;
I have been there to walk—
even in winter there are groves
of red canes
to spice the bleached meadows,

small spiders dash across the path,
the footing is rough,
but under bent weeds your name murmurs in a brook
and sings in wind that flies ahead to lead me
willingly

to ask you what you have seen,
knowing it is the same
as what I love.
And now a blue break in the clouds: the grasses glow
at their tips.

In March

Orion sinks behind the ridge
the owl's voice opens
she is dusted blue in the moonlight
in early spring
there is a sound her heart desires
like the wind
in dry weeds revealing a presence
that is ancient

how many times has this owl
told the tops of pines
counted the stars between pine needles
the hunter she is yearns
for a sound to trigger her launch and glide
to seize a small thing
to fulfill this night

the spark of the senses
in stars in the silence
staring into the deep
familiar night always new
full of wings of life and death
of clouds crossing the moon

High Desert Grasses

Raddled and pale
they show their need

bow to it   break from it
its dry taste and garment of dust

that wind threatens to tear away
so little have they

when I rest in these grasses
they poke me sharply

probe under my cuffs to scratch
and reach for my face

until I shift   allowing them
to raise their heads slowly

jealous of my body
its shadow   and water

its freedom   they cannot grasp
their presence against me   blades

Alphabet of Passing

A half rainbow against alkali clouds
makes a flag of joy
for the eye
no matter that my hand
is empty

shoulders of snowy mist move
down from the western
slopes
as old snags
and scraps of burnt bark

let go finger by finger
and sink
colorless now
no longer burning
and the half rainbow fades

clouds of dust and moisture together
turn and turn like an ancient gray beast
compressing a sleep den
gathering its mind
into its own center

the night comes in snowfall
no one
will breach the covering
neither mouse nor human foot
leaves its alphabet of passing

Part IV: Things I Want

After the Equinox

As the sun one day crosses a line
that has been drawn in everybody's mind
and dry leaves leap across the ground crust,
their backbones already cracked by frost,
I find the huge bolus of the paper wasps'
nest abandoned by my small enemies.

The lesson here, of course, is that you wait.
The old will to poison with a touch
curls up and drops next to the porch
like a scatter of planed chips. The late
great power that lent so much
purpose to this world on the camellia branch

has failed of breath in October's grip.
Wasp corpses scuff on the stoop. It's time
to sweep away their deaths. When I step out,
broom in hand, the yellow twists take
one last swirl at my feet, but I'm
the stronger now. Watch me, watch me sweep.

Winter, Weather, Water, White

—at play in the Oxford English Dictionary

i.

Winter's
A condition to endure and suffer from,
Whittle it down to basic white.
Amid the breakers during a storm
A ship may behave well or ill. That
Is its weather.

ii.

The winter rains.
It makes fair weather to tilt the tiller
For trim against the winds.
Slant the sails of a windmill to resist its axis.
A surface sloped to divert gulleywash
Will wear its exposure.

iii.

Water's more to tell.
Cold vapor fills
The district around a river,
Streams or rifts a hunter's horse must leap.
False capital that slides through one's grip,
It names whole quarters

Of the world.
No taste in the sip

Of water that whitens a pearl,
But in the flush in green liquor.
Childhood's game: water-my-chickens, come-cheep.
The gambler's knuckle.

iv.

Go down the weather, bankrupt,
Or stretch wing to weather, fly.
Winter's a narrow board,
a white grip of ice holding this new year.
It hardens, it seasons. Try
The late-ripening fruit.

Filamentous

Filamentous, flexible feathers
Are avian attributes.
Bills bore, break, abrade
And tear, with talons, tips
Sharp in shape for slashing,
Gripping, gouging,
Proving
No Pretty Polly.

Gizzards gather grit and
Grind grain,
Whereas wings wield their
Wearers through weather,
Wilds, waters, wherever.
Long-legged birds
Lean over their evenly divided
Limbs. Loons'
Feet aft flail them forward to fish
In deep dives,

Tree-sitters' tendons tighten
On twigs,
Bark, or branches,
The hallux holding hard.
Adaptive to their eating, aerial
Although not always,
Plungers, parasitic pirates,
Skuas, skimmers and slim-standing
Stripe-necked
Or splay-stepping,

Birds may strain sea brine

Or adjust uneven ears
Over evening hours to hear
Rodents rustle, or may, rarely,
Consume clods of clay,
Muddy minerals.
A tube tongue, some have, long as a tong
For bright blossoms, and some
Snatch bees from the air.

O to know more, the agility, ability,
Migratory amazements, the secret
Dinosaurs, the omens, catapults
Straight up from water,
Deep bore of a stork bill,
Its ancient calculating eye,
Cacophony, the singing world,
The creak of a hinge voice
Hidden in river reeds,
A hunter slipping its jess.

Happy in the Way of Older Women

—against "A Poem of Towers," by James Wright

If I am becoming one of the old women,
I will leave my chair rocking alone in the light
that falls past open blinds, when a cardinal
takes off from its branch.

The old women, he says, are happy
in a way he does not understand. But he
is a man. When the electricity goes out
do women gather darkness

into their laps? Winter evenings
sometimes do not require light beyond that
of leftover snow and the moon, the cold
flavors of dormant grass.

My bones speak more these days
like older women's, about the clouds that spread paint
across the western horizon, with its
five layers of water

and its delicate borders between ice
and the creek's surface, which moves away
in its same place. For me, it's time
when the migrant

birds wing in with a lengthening day,
I choose what will fit into my pockets,
one song, and worn and well-fitting
old shoes.

Flavor of Roses

I meant to choose chocolate, but it was a slow night
At a Middle Eastern restaurant in Paris, and the owner
Chatted with me while his children played near the back wall

Or approached with amber eyes at table height to watch
This strange American off the beaten path, eating
Rice and goat meat, flat bread. The night was mild for winter,

And I suppose windows shone high over this tiny alley
Where the restaurant squeezed between walls. There may
Have been rain. Dessert arrived before I could say "chocolate"

And I didn't notice, talk flowed, then the owner beamed
As I tasted the soft green custard. It scented my mouth,
Filled my nostrils with familiar aroma. A specialty,

He nodded. Rose petals. I closed my eyes,
Rolled the wrong dessert over my tongue, let it suffuse
My thoughts, at the rickety table, in France, in January,

All of us far from home, the smiling and curious family,
The essence of warm flowers, and me, spending
My last francs on *le menu prix fixe.*

Breathing Tea

Breathe deeply: mist over
The tea, its scents evoke
The ruffled hills of
Nara, over the river,
Hills exhaling morning,
Small wild creatures awakening
Amid leaves,

Understory
Of deep greens in patterns
Varied as kimono, slits of
Sunlight, filtered, as if in heated
Water, releasing the essence
Of minerals, a taste
Of tender black mushrooms.

My nose in the cup, I
Inhale hungrily. I cannot
Help it, my eyes close,
I dream into the gloom under
The shade canopy, delve
Toward the low tea plants
Palm-open, taking and giving
The hillsides' riches

As earth-smell rises
Between old leaves and tracks
Of worms beloved of the tea
Plants, the casings, a tang
Of decay,
This one spot of terroir
Complex and rich as fur.

Whicker

Horse talk in my ear: I wish I had it,
would love to hear the glottal air
whistle in the long throat,
the horse's ear cocked to track me,
its head sideways, near mine.

I wish not to be afraid
of the ponderous hooves shifting,
the great muscles standing easily,
heavily,
over my shoulder, beside my ear,
the casual power.

It is grace
to feel easy around a horse.
I envy the gift in my niece:
she can look in the horse's eyes
with her spirit, see its spirit
of the wind through trees and meadows.

When I fly
it's a phantom of dreams.
When she flies it is real,
something that lifts her willingly
and keeps going because
they both want to,

and once only
a distant horse saw me and mistook
my shape, and whinnied loudly
in greeting; I waved and called out
to let it know I was not

the right human

but I appreciated
the thought.

The Tree Surgeon Dreams of Bowling

Up in the highest joint that holds my weight
against shifting breezes, I dance my hips
while keeping both feet planted, one on a limb,
the other in the crevice of an old scar.
Twigs with five-leaf fingers stroke
my cheek, then slap when I lift
the cutting tool and let it bite.

That tree-hand falls away, and I look up
into fresh light, release the safety, let
the blade-buzz decrescendo
like applause fading. I seem to be standing
at the line, one arm cocked back and heavy
gripping my favorite bowling ball,
the one marbled with iridescent green,
its old surface chipped
from years of small-town teams

rolling in on Thursday nights,
thirty frames or so, and we'd grind a tiny pencil
to write a 7, an 8, a 6, an X now and then.
But here, in this aging pear tree, my legs splayed wide,
my arm aches from the tool's vibrations—
going nowhere but cutting away
things I wish I didn't need.

Down

Don't talk down to me. I'm not in a hole or under the bed
or beneath the car's back bumper,

Not tucked under beige wads of grasses gone dormant
from lack of rain, nor have I slipped

Behind the clothes hamper unseen, like a single sock.
I'm not down in the mouth or down East,

I'm here, not downtown under a downspout downing a drink
in a down jacket. Don't talk at all

If down is the way you're planning to go. I hope you understand
I'm laying down the law.

Things I Want

peace of mind   silence when I want to think
thoughts when I want to think   of mind
a piece of my mind can be a lovely thing
a bright red net that sifts the air
with no need to catch butterflies   and butterflies are here

temperate days for walking outdoors barefoot
if possible   barefoot's a state of mind
sidewalk and soft gravel prickling and sliding
under toe pads   sand underfoot too pushes back
and rolls with the heel and arch and ball joints
close to the muscle

some breeze to cool the skin   so the day fits my body

not being thirsty or hungry or worried
the realization of not being in want
is something I want
that thought   lightly landing on the back of my hand
before it lifts off   I stand here perfectly   happy

From the Perseids

Desire spins in our arms as we embrace,
And also in the night sky

In August, month of cicada buzz, a longing
That scrapes the stars'

Sharp edges as constellations swing in circles,
Our lips, hands

Stretching across rounded landscapes in the darkness.
Falling

Into our space suddenly, the asteroids flash their tails
In the northwest

And plunge toward rooftops, toward tree crowns, like handfuls
Of jacks tossed

In a moon's game, their silver shoestrings trailing brightly
For a few seconds.

Which streak will take over the whole sky, be so long
We loose our voices

To call the name of that shooting star, the arc
That shears across the sky?

Everywhere After All

—after "so you want to be a writer?" by Charles Bukowski

It is everywhere after all,
in the crushed stones of the macadam,
in the pearls of dirt eaten by worms
if you have good soil,

in the fractures of church window glass
rampant with color,
in the multiplicity of a lark's smallest
feathers

and the seed hulls left in white droppings.
It traces constellations
into fantastic animals
flexing, flowing, and always

on the hunt, between the thieving fingers
of sycamore branches in winter
when naked means hunger.
Lose track

of yourself in a mosaic
that eats your mind. It is all true.
Baby, would I lie to you?
Never.

In and Out of Rough Water

Barks of sea lions are carried on the wind.
At cliff's edge, I look down into

The cauldron of the Pacific Ocean
Where sleek skullcaps in the breakers

Ride low, skim under foam, as the sea
Flexes its muscles against Oregon's shore.

Submarine shadows flow and vanish
In the element of their lives.

Some dark shapes turn to the boulders
And haul out awkwardly, heavy bodies slipping,

Their flippers and tails slapping,
Their efforts a clamor of yelps.

Some fall back into the surf,
The punishing necessity that bursts

Over jagged rocks, withdraws, the medium
Of anticipation and fulfillment, negotiation

Of an endless hunger. I want to understand
How the sea lions decide

Where to struggle back up
Onto the black rocks, when to enter the water again,

How to give their bodies to the sea's—to learn
To inhabit wildness and feed from it,

How to rise through those thrilling, drowning waves.

About the Author

Jayne Marek's poems and art photos appear in publications such as *Spillway, Camas, Gravel, Blast Furnace, New Mexico Review, Gyroscope, Peacock Journal, Central American Literary Review, Lantern Journal, Siren, Flying Island,* and *Tipton Poetry Journal*; she twice provided color cover art and black-and-white pictures for *The Bend*. Her prior collections are *Company of Women: New and Selected Poems* (co-authored with Lylanne Musselman and Mary Sexson, 2013), and *Imposition of Form on the Natural World* (2013). She has received two fellowships from the National Endowment for the Humanities for literary scholarship and two Pushcart Prize nominations for poetry. She was also a finalist for the David Martinson–Meadowhawk Prize. Her one-act play "Katherine and Virginia," which characterizes the friendship between authors Katherine Mansfield and Virginia Woolf, has been performed in New York City and Indiana. A professor emerita of English (Ph.D. University of Wisconsin) who also holds an M.F.A. (the University of Notre Dame), she now makes her home in the Pacific Northwest, near the wild and beautiful coast, where she writes, photographs, and learns about natural history.

www.ingramcontent.com/pod-product-compliance
Lightning Source LLC
Chambersburg PA
CBHW071101090426
42737CB00013B/2421

* 9 7 8 1 9 4 5 7 5 2 2 9 2 *